FISH OUT OF WATER

FISH OUT OF WATER

Nazi Submariners as Prisoners in North Louisiana during World War II

WESLEY HARRIS

RoughEdge Publications

Printed in the United States of America

Library of Congress Control No. 2004095452
ISBN 0-9666889-2-9

RoughEdge Publications
P O Box 30
Ruston, LA   71273-0030

roughedge57@yahoo.com

FISH OUT OF WATER

World War II brought change to the small north Louisiana town of Ruston.

Ruston contributed its share of young men to the armed services, some leaving mother and farm for the first time. Blue star banners adorned windows and Victory gardens filled back yards. The local college, Louisiana Tech, was the site of a Navy V-12 program for training young Naval and Marine officers.

Patriotic fervor was high. Paper drives, rubber drives, and scrap metal drives allowed everyone to contribute to the war effort.

Perhaps the most visible change to the community was the introduction of thousands of enemy prisoners into one of the 155 POW base camps or 511 smaller branch camps established across America. Camp Ruston was erected in a frenzy of construction. In a matter of months, barracks, barbed wire, and guard towers replaced cotton stalks and pine trees.

The most interesting of these prisoners would be the Nazi submarine sailors from at least three different German U-boats. With these sailors came military secrets and mysteries which were not revealed for decades.

Fish out of water, these young men from the sea had to adjust to the sweltering, mosquito infested hills of north Louisiana, their fate unknown to their families in Germany. But humane treatment by the camp's guards and the kindness shown by the locals not only made their imprisonment tolerable, but prompted many to immigrate to the United States after the war.

CAMP RUSTON CREATED

Prisoner of war camps were established in the United States following the defeat of Field Marshal Erwin Rommel's Afrika Korps by the British 8th Army in Tunisia in May 1943. The capture of several hundred thousand German troops complicated an already critical shortage of prison space in England. The United Kingdom begged the United States to take on the burden, and the War Department reluctantly agreed.

Front gate of Camp Ruston

At the beginning of World War II, the United States had no prisoner internment camps in existence or under construction. An extensive building campaign resulted in POW camps in 46 of the 48 states, holding a total of 375,000 German POWs, or PWs as they were called then.

After capture, all prisoners entered the United States through two points of embarkation—Camp Shanks, New York or Norfolk, Virginia. From these points, POWs were processed and distributed to one of the main camps or smaller branch camps. Most camps were located in the South or Southwest, far from critical war industries.

The POW camps were generally segregated by branch of service, rank, or political affiliation. POWs identified as "hard core" Nazis were held separately from other populations. Camp Ruston would be designated an "anti-Nazi" camp. Camp Clinton, Mississippi held nearly forty generals and three admirals during the war. Officers and enlisted men were divided into separate compounds. Some camps contained predominantly Afrika Corps, Luftwaffe [Air Force], Army, or naval personnel.

Most of the camps were designated as extensions of existing military bases, but in Louisiana, Camps Livingston and Polk were determined to be too small. After scouting locations in several parishes, a site in north central Louisiana was chosen for a new internment facility—Camp Ruston.

Sprawling over 750 acres, Camp Ruston was built in accordance with layout plans which had been standardized by the War Department. The T. L. James Company of Ruston was awarded the building contract at a cost of $2,500,000.

Camp Ruston's recreation hall

Construction began in September 1942 and was completed in time for the camp's dedication on Christmas Day 1942. Camp Ruston would be one of five major POW Camps in Louisiana.

The camp initially consisted of three compounds, identical rectangular enclosures, 1170 feet by 710 feet. Each compound was designed to accommodate one battalion of 1,600 PWs. Each compound was subdivided into four companies of 400 prisoners. Each company consisted of eight barracks, one latrine, one mess hall, and a company storehouse and a recreation building.

Each prisoner compound also had an infirmary, a canteen, a workshop, and a battalion administration building. The compounds were accessible by asphalt roads called compound streets which divided the enclosures lengthwise.

The compounds were enclosed by two barbed wire fences, ten feet high and sixteen feet apart, which encircled the internment area and the hospital complex. Guard towers, approximately twenty feet tall, stood strategically along the outer fence. A vehicle patrol road, twenty-two feet wide, ran outside and parallel to the double fence.

Since the camp was literally carved out of the piney woods, a complete water and sewer system had to be laid. Three wells were dug to provide water and a large water tower was constructed.

In addition to the prisoner compounds, the camp included a large hospital, administrative offices, a post exchange, and barracks for the military police companies guarding the prisoners. The camp also boasted a large recreation hall and gymnasium.

Much smaller satellite camps under the auspices of Camp Ruston were established near other north

Louisiana military compounds in communities like Bastrop and Tallulah.

Guard tower overlooking Camp Ruston

WAACS
The first inhabitants of Camp Ruston were not enemy prisoners but American women. Due to the initial slow influx of captured soldiers, the facility first served as a basic training base for the Women's Army Auxiliary Corps. In March 1943, Camp Ruston was activated as Branch "A" of the 5th Women's Army

Auxiliary Corps Training Center under the condition that group toilets and showers and other "masculine-type plumbing" would not be modified and that the WAACs "would move out on a 30 days notice if German and Italian prisoners should need the place."

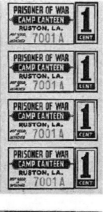

No. of Dependents........1........
CASH ONLY   **Nº   .161**
SALES COMMISSARY
PRISONER OF WAR CAMP, RUSTON, LA.

Pvt. Samuel O. Gibbs

Name, Rank, Organization

is authorized to make cash purchases at the Sales Store upon presentation of this card.

Void after..1/1/45....   C/LORD F. LINCOLN
                 Date   1st LT., Q. M. C.
Pvt. Samuel O. Gibbs   Sales Officer
Signature of Customer   Sales Officer

Commissary ID card for soldier stationed at Camp Ruston

Coupons used as money at Camp Ruston

6

The 5th WAAC headquarters was established in the unused old high school building in downtown Ruston, with additional training facilities at Camp Monticello, Arkansas and Camp Polk, Louisiana. Member of the staff were housed at the Ruston Hotel and in local homes.

In April 1943, the first 500 recruits arrived at Camp Ruston to form the 42nd WAAC Regiment. In greeting the young women, the regimental commander reminded them, "Now you're a soldier," and went on to explain the rules of army life and discipline. He encouraged them to dedicate themselves to their training and "take it like a soldier."

In many respects, the training was similar to that received by combat soldiers. The basic training course included infantry drill, physical training, military customs and courtesies, defense against chemical attack, and WAAC regulations. Days were filled with a detailed schedule of drills, calisthenics, and classes. Optional classes in Spanish and German were held in the evenings.

Some recruits received specialized training in motor transport to become drivers of jeeps and trucks and make minor repairs to military vehicles. About 160 WAACs completed a cooks' and bakers' school.

Local residents provided a warm welcome to the recruits, setting up a USO center that would later serve the camp guards as well as Marines and sailors participating in Louisiana Tech's V-12 officer training program. Civic clubs set up day rooms around the camp and local churches furnished the chapel.

Although the training operation was large, it was short-lived. In three and a half months, 2,277 WAAC recruits received basic training. The close of the training program coincided with the redesignation of the WAAC as the Women's Army Corps (WAC), part of the regular Army. By July, the WACs were gone with prisoners on the way.

THE AFRIKA KORPS ARRIVES

On 14 August 1943, 300 enlisted men from Rommel's elite Afrika Korps arrived to become Camp Ruston's first internees. The flow of prisoners continued and by October reached a peak population of 4,315 men (including 181 officers), all of whom were Afrika Korps veterans. Over the next two years, troops from other army units and the Luftwaffe would be added.

German prisoners march into Camp Ruston

The Camp's three original compounds grew full resulting in the addition of a fourth compound for officers only in the far north west section of the camp.

Camp Ruston consisted of over 360 buildings and at its peak housed over 5,000 American military and prisoner personnel, a population equal to a small city. The camp brought together the most remarkable mixture of nationalities every assembled in one place in the history of the state of Louisiana. While Germans made up most of the prisoner complement, many nationalities were represented. Italians, Poles, Russians, Poles, Yugoslavians, Latvians, Spaniards, Hungarians, Czechs, Vichy French, Austrians, Dutch, Danish, Mongolians and even American nationals comprised the camp population. The highest ranking prisoner to be kept at Camp Ruston was German Brigadier General Hans Gaul.

American Army troops of the Eighth Service Command guarded Camp Ruston

When asked to describe Camp Ruston, Rudolf Beyer, a former Luftwaffe fighter pilot responded, "It was a tough Camp but by German standards it was still like a vacation. We had good food, just the standard issue American food as prescribed by the Geneva Convention. The professional cooks that we had among the prisoners made an excellent dinner out of it.

"As a newcomer, it was real tough for you. They didn't trust new comers. You had the old Camp establishment, the ones that had been there for two years. There were cliques ruling the Camp... Political ones, I was even investigated by one group controlled by a communist, very powerful, like a commissar (a Communist Party leader). They wanted to know why I didn't throw my flying boots away. "

Beyer was probably referring to a soldier from the 999th Afrikan Division, a German military unit composed former concentration camp internees. A large number of 999th troops were interned at Camp Ruston. German concentration camps originally served to reeducate German citizens that were deemed unfriendly to the Nazi party. These internees were often intellectuals, socialists, communists or members and leaders of labor unions or rival political parties. Many of these "reeducated" Germans were placed in the 999th to fight for Germany.

In late 1939, as a 17-year old living with his immigrant German parents in Yakima, Washington, Ludwig Staudinger, sought the excitement of war and returned to Germany to fight for the Third Reich.

Little did he know that the U.S. would join the war and that he would later become a prisoner of the Americans with many other German soldiers as an enemy POW. His letters to his parents while he was a PW at Camp Ruston tell of his misfortune and realization of his boyhood mistake.

In a letter dated 21 July 1944, young Staudinger wrote his parents in Yakima, "I want you to know that I left the Prussian war machine as I had joined it; voluntarily, sadder, for having given three years of my youth but much wiser." Later, in August, he penned, "I realized too late the mistake I had made in not listening to your advice to stay in the U.S.A. I often thank God that you were not there, it is truly no place for decent people, seeing is believing and I saw plenty."

In September 1944, Staudinger was still kicking himself for leaving the U.S. to join the Nazi Army: "I consider myself world sucker No. 1 for having ever gone back to that infernal country. I was in Russia most of the time, however on furlough in Munich the sight of those gluttonous Nazi big-wigs almost made me vomit. The idiotic lies in the propaganda sheets were ridiculous beyond words. Better to be a man without a country than to be a German."

Aerial view of the asphalt road surrounding Camp Ruston and double barbed wire fence and guard towers

RUSTON'S ENIGMA SECRET

In late summer 1944, the captured crew of the German submarine *U-505* arrived at Camp Ruston. Brought in by night, with no other prisoners, they would be segregated from the others for some time.

Mary Duchaney, a civilian employee at the camp, remembered the crew's arrival. She was a nurse at the hospital and helped process the sailors into the camp. "I was sworn to secrecy and couldn't tell anyone about their presence."

The sailors were placed in an unused compound of the camp. Efforts were taken to conceal their identity from the other prisoners and civilians as well. There was good reason for the secrecy.

In his book *Hitler's U-boat War*, Clay Blair calls the *U-505* "the sorriest U-boat in the Atlantic force," referring to over a dozen aborted patrols between December 1942 and March 1944. One *U-505* captain even committed suicide by shooting himself in the head under the stress of a depth charge attack. When the *505* was able to engage in its mission, it was highly successful. Before its capture, *U-505* carried out twelve patrols with eight ships sunk for a total of 44,962 tons sent to the bottom of the sea.

Laid down on 12 June 1940, the U-boat was commissioned on 26 August 1941. It was 252 feet long and had a displacement of 1,100 tons. It carried 21 torpedoes and had a crew of four officers and 56 men. Its surface speed was 18 knots and its submerged speed was six to seven knots. The deepest it could dive was down to 600 feet. Four different officers commanded the *U-505* during its short service.

U-505 was captured at sea on 4 June 1944, by the U.S. Navy Task Force 22.3 off the west coast of Africa. Led by the U.S.S. *Guadalcanal*, the American warships launched an intensive depth charge attack that forced the *U-505* to surface.

Hans Goebeler, a control room operator on the *U-505,* would later describe the fierce attack on his submarine:

"One depth charge was so close it damaged torpedoes stored in the upper deck. Other depth charges jammed our main rudder and diving planes. Soon there was nothing for us to do but surface and abandon ship before she sank for good."

As the U-boat surfaced, American destroyers and aircraft raked it with machine gun fire. One *U-505* sailor was killed and several wounded.

Harald Lange, *505's* commander, described what it was like on the surface:

"When the boat surfaced, I was the first on the bridge and saw now four destroyers around me, shooting at my boat with caliber and anti-aircraft. The nearest one, in now through 110 degrees, was shooting with shrapnel into the conning tower. I got wounded by numerous shots and shrapnel in both knees and legs and fell down. At once I gave the order to leave the boat and to sink her. My chief officer, who came after me onto the bridge, lay on the starboard side with blood streaming over his face. Then I gave a course order to starboard in order to make the aft part of the conning tower fire lee at the destroyer to get my crew out of the boat safely. I lost consciousness for I don't know how long, but when I awoke again a lot of my men were on the deck and I made an effort to raise myself and haul myself aft. By the explosion of a shell I was blown from the first antiaircraft deck down onto the main deck; the explosion hit near the starboard machine gun.

"I saw a lot of my men running on the main deck, getting pipe boats [individual life rafts] clear. In a conscious moment, I gave notice to the chief that I was still on the main deck. How I got over the side I don't know exactly, but I suppose by another explosion. Despite my injuries I somehow managed to keep afloat until two members of my group brought a pipe boat and hoisted me into it; my lifejacket had been punctured with shrapnel and was no good. During all this time I could not see much because in the first seconds of the fight I had been hit in the face and eye with splinters of wood blasted from the deck; my right eyelid was pierced with a splinter."

Photo taken from a Navy plane shows the U-505 crew abandoning ship

Lange gave the order to abandon *U-505* and to scuttle her to prevent the U-boat's capture. Hans Goebeler was the only German sailor to make an effort to sink the sub by opening the sea strainer cover so water would flood in and send the boat to the bottom. He then joined his comrades in the ocean.

"The destroyers and planes were giving us hell," Goebeler would later write in a book, "firing weapons at our boat. We swam away from the sub as quickly as possible. The planes were shooting the water between us and the boat, chasing us away from *U-505*. Only the very front of the boat and the top of the conning tower was still above the water. The American skipper must have had some men who were very brave, or very crazy, because they boarded the sub, found the sea strainer cover and closed it."

A boarding party from the U.S.S. *Pillsbury* closed in before the *U-505* could slide below the surface. In a feat of expert seamanship by a crew of mostly teenagers, the *U-505* was rescued from a watery grave. Captain (later Admiral) Daniel Gallery, commander of the U.S. task force, described the dangerous task of taking over the *U-505*:

"The sub was left running at about 10 knots with her rudder jammed hard right and in just about full surface trim. The *Pillsbury's* boat had to chase the sub and cut inside the circle to catch her, which she did, and the boarding party, consisting of eight enlisted men and Lieutenant (j.g. [junior grade]) Albert Leroy David, leaped from the boat to the circling sub and took possession of it.

"On deck there was one dead man. They didn't know what was down below. They had every reason to believe, from the way the sub was still running, that there were still Nazis left below engaged in scuttling, setting booby traps or perhaps getting rid of confidential gear. At any rate David and two enlisted men, one named Knispel, the other Wdowiak, plunged down the conning tower hatch carrying hand grenades and machine guns ready to fight it out with anyone they found below. They very definitely put their lives on the line when they went down the hatch. However, they found no one below.

"They did find that water was pouring into the U-boat through a bilge strainer about eight inches in diameter which had the cover knocked off, and that all the vents were open and the boat was rapidly flooding. When they found there was no one else below they called the other boarders below and went to work closing vents. They found the cover to this bilge strainer, slapped it back in place, screwed up the butterfly nuts on it and checked the flooding, just in the nick of time."

Captured *U-505* submariners held at gunpoint

The *U-505* became the first man-of-war captured on the high seas by the U.S. Navy since 1815. For their heroism, Lt. David received the Medal of Honor and seamen Wdowiak and Knispel the Navy Cross. Seven American sailors received the Silver Star.

Fifty-nine Nazi sailors were seized; 56 were sent to Camp Ruston. *(See U.S. Navy documents in the Appendix for more information on the U-505's capture.)*

Although the seizure of an enemy vessel was a major accomplishment, the true value in the capture of the *U-505* lay in the discovery of an Enigma code machine and codes used by the German navy to communicate.

The Enigma machine was an advanced electro-mechanical cipher device developed in Germany after

American sailors struggle to save the *U-505*

World War I. Enigma was used by all branches of the German military as their main instrument for secure wireless communications until the end of World War II. Several models of the Enigma machine were developed before and during World War II, each more complex and harder to code-break than its predecessors. The most complex Enigma model was used by the German navy.

The basic operating procedure of the Enigma machine was simple. To send an encrypted message, the operator set the Enigma's electric and mechanical settings (the plug wirings and the rotor wheels) to a predefined initial combination known to him and to the receiving operator. Then he typed the free text message on the keyboard. For each typed letter, a different letter was lit in the upper board. The operator wrote down each lit letter, so that when he finished typing the original message on the Enigma, he had a meaningless stream of letters, which was the encrypted message. He then transmitted the encrypted message with a standard Morse code radio transmitter. The receiving operator wrote the received encrypted message, set his Enigma machine to the same pre-defined combination, and then typed the message on the machine's keyboard. Typing the encrypted message with the same combination of settings deciphered it, so the operator could read the original free text message by the letters lit in the upper board as he typed.

Enigma code machine

By mid-1940, work by the Allies had allowed code-breakers to read some German army Enigma messages, but the most important German Enigma messages, those of the U-boat submarines, could not be deciphered. The code-breakers needed more information about the German navy's Enigma, its operating procedures, and its settings. This information could only be obtained by capturing German ships and submarines at sea. The German navy considered the possibility a vessel might be boarded by the enemy, and made preparations to prevent the capture of Enigma machines and documents. The devices were designed so the most critical parts could be removed quickly and thrown into the sea. Steps were taken to make it easy for a sub crew to sink its damaged U-boat as it was abandoned.

Because of the discovery of the secret naval codes and the technology of a new acoustic torpedo on board the *U-505,* the crew members were secretly shipped to Camp Ruston where they were held incommunicado. Secrecy was essential for the capture of the Enigma machine and codes to have any value.

Sailor Otto Dietz would later write about the journey to Camp Ruston:

"In Norfolk [Virginia] we were all interrogated. There we received black POW uniforms. From the docks we were taken under heavy security to a railroad train—our windows were nailed shut, and after a two-day trip we reached the POW camp in Ruston, Louisiana. It must have been about the middle of July 1944."

One former camp employee recalled that the *U-505* crew arrived by train at about three o'clock in the morning. Eulis Carroll was surprised that most of the sailors were teenagers. As part of the medical staff,

Carroll aided in giving the crew physical exams before admittance into the camp. He noted the sailors had no clue where they were and probably had no idea they were so far from the sea.

In a memo from the War Department, the Provost Marshal General, responsible for all POWs across the country, received this directive:

1. Reference is made to fifty six (56) German Naval prisoners of war [four (4) officers and fifty two (52) enlisted men] now at Camp Ruston, Louisiana. It is important that these particular prisoners of war not be allowed to mingle or communicate with any other prisoners of war at any time. Necessary provisions will be made to insure that no communications of any nature from this group of prisoners reach Germany.

2. No reports of capture of members of this group of Naval prisoners of war will be submitted either to the protecting power or to the International Red Cross without specific authorization.

3. This confirms verbal instructions issued to Brigadier General B.M. Bryan, Jr.

BY DIRECTION OF THE CHIEF OF STAFF.

When the International Red Cross visited Camp Ruston, it was refused admittance into the *U-505* compound. An IRC representative wrote in his report, "the commander did not permit us to visit one of the sections containing 50 prisoners, and our efforts to visit this section failed. Admission to this section was forbidden to civilians by superior authorities, even to representatives of the Committee of the International Red Cross."

After another visit, the Red Cross inspector wrote in his March 1945 report:

"The last one [compound] is occupied by naval officers which we are not allowed to visit as was the case at the time of the preceding visit in spite of representations made before the War Department."

Even later, the efforts to keep the *U-505's* capture a secret continued. On 26 April 1945, a Captain Burke ordered a Captain Winkenhofer to:

"Inform the 8th SvC [Service Command, the Army unit in charge of Camp Ruston] *that under no circumstances should the Swiss representatives be permitted to ascertain that these Navy prisoners are at Ruston. In other words, move the boys out of Ruston before the Swiss arrive and then return them to Ruston as soon as the Swiss depart."*

Officers of the *U-505*

Eventually, many of the *U-505* sailors were assigned to work crews around Ruston. In his book *Steel Boats, Iron Hearts*, Hans Goebeler recalled the rough work on local farms:

"...the backbreaking labor cured me of all my Jack London-inspired fantasies about the romantic life of lumbermen. Picking cotton was even more odious. The cotton flowers tore at one's fingers, and the constant stooping and bending was agonizing."

Goebeler performed most of his farm labor for a Ruston farmer named Simonton. Goebeler said Simonton was "a fine old gentleman and we became quite good friends. In fact, he told me that if I returned to Ruston after the war, he would adopt me as his son! He said I would make a fine farmer and would be a credit to the community." I was deeply touched by his offer, but I told him I had a family back in Germany and that they would need me to get through the tough times ahead."

Despite their isolation, the *U-505* sailors were treated well. Otto Dietz wrote:

"We were placed in a large isolated part of (the camp), so that we would not be able to see any other POW's. Our relatives at home were informed we were killed.

"Our life in the camp was very pleasant—we received regular U.S. Army rations which our cook prepared for us at the kitchen barracks. Our salary was 80 cents a day without our having to work. This was a great deal of money since in our canteen everything was very inexpensive—a pack of cigarettes costs ten cents; soft drink, five cents; beer (Falstaff), fifteen cents. Our five officers including Commander Lange came in September to join us and had their own barracks. There were so many barracks there that for the 52 of us, there was plenty of room. We converted one of the barracks into a bowling alley and we also had other barracks in which beautiful movies were shown."

In 1954, nearly a decade after the war ended, the *U-505* was acquired by the Museum of Science and Industry in Chicago and placed on exhibit. In April 2004, the *505* moved from its outdoor display site where it had suffered from the elements for fifty years to a new indoor multimillion dollar exhibit hall. It is one of only five remaining U-boats in the world, attracting over a million visitors to Chicago annually.

U-505 sailors in a Ruston cotton field

U-664

On 1 November 1942, another German submarine, the *U-664,* set out on her maiden patrol, captained by Adolf Graef, 26. She was severely damaged by depth charges dropped by a Catalina aircraft of U.S. Navy Squadron VP-84, and had to abort to France. After repairs, *U-664* participated in five patrols, scoring three ships sunk for a total of 19,325 tons.

On 6 August 1943, the U.S. Navy, using radio direction finding, located *U-664* during its mission of refueling other U-boats as it transferred fuel oil to *U-262* by means of a water hose. Radio traffic between five U-boats in the area kept U.S. Navy ships and aircraft close for the next several days as the subs secreted themselves under the water.

On the morning of 8 August, *U-664* passed the water hose to *U-760* while *U-262* lay on the surface nearby. During the fuel transfer, Wildcat and Avenger aircraft from the U.S.S. *Card* appeared and attacked all three subs. The U-boats remained on the surface to fight. The Wildcat sprayed the subs with machine gun fire, killing *664's* second watch officer and a coxswain who had run on deck to disconnect the hose. The Navy Wildcat was riddled by return fire and the pilot killed. The Avenger dropped two depth charges but the plane was raked by fire, killing the radioman and forcing the pilot to ditch in the water.

Later that night, *664* spotted the *Card* as it arrived on the scene. Graef fired three torpedoes, but missed the *Card*, diving deep to avoid the subsequent depth charge attack.

At noon on 9 August, the *U-664* surfaced to air the boat and charge batteries. Again the U-boat was caught on the surface by a Wildcat and two Avengers from the *Card*. The Avengers dropped bombs and depth charges, forcing the *U-664* crew to abandon ship.

The *U-664* under attack

The American planes did their best to rescue survivors by dropping rafts and life vests and calling the U.S.S. *Borie* to the scene. In the eight hours until the *Borie* arrived, *U-664* crewman Horst Blumenberg found himself at the bottom of a raft, covered with the blood and bodies of his wounded comrades. When the *Borie* did arrive, American sailors fired into the water. After surviving bombs and depth charges and hours adrift without aid, Blumenberg suddenly thought, "Don't tell me after all this, I'm going to get shot."

While the *Borie* was searching for survivors, the *U-262* launched five torpedoes at the destroyer, forcing it to leave the area without recovering eight members of the *U-664* crew. Forty-four survivors were taken to Casablanca, Morocco and eventually found their way to Fort Meade, Maryland and later Fort Hunt, Virginia for interrogations.

Horst Blumenberg was the only member of the *U-664* crew to be sent to Camp Ruston. Blumenberg had declared himself an anti-Nazi at Fort Meade and was separated from the rest of the crew and assigned to Ruston's "anti-Nazi" camp. Most of the others went to Papago Park, a camp for hardcore Nazis just outside Phoenix, Arizona.

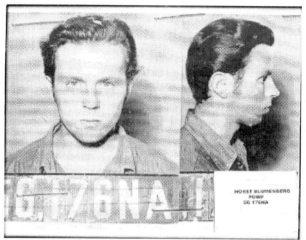

Horst Blumenberg

U-234

One of the biggest submarine mysteries of World War II centers on the last voyage of the *U-234*. With the end of war drawing near, the captain and crew of the *U-234* decided to surrender to the United States Navy than attempt its ambitious mission of delivering a top secret cargo to Japan.

Of the approximately sixty crew members who gave themselves up, only one, 22-year old Karl Ernst Pfaff was sent to Camp Ruston. What was on the *U-*

234 and why only one sailor was sent to Ruston remained classified for many years.

Departing Germany in late March 1945, *U-234's* mission was to deliver some of Germany's best military technology to Japan. Originally a mine-laying submarine, the *U-234* was three times the size of the standard attack U-boat. Its huge cargo included V-2 rocket and jet fighter components, and about 1,200 pounds of uranium oxide needed in Japan's own atomic weapons program. After weeks of evading Allied attacks, the ship's crew surrendered to the U.S. Navy upon learning of Germany's impending defeat. The ship was escorted to an American port and its cargo carefully scrutinized. The uranium oxide, however, quickly vanished without a trace.

John Lansdale, an official in the U.S. atomic bomb program called the Manhattan Project, contends the uranium was sent to America's own bomb-building program where it found its way into the devices dropped on Hiroshima and Nagasaki. At the time, Lansdale was an Army lieutenant colonel for intelligence and security for the atom bomb project.

Lansdale's assertion raises the possibility that the atomic weapons that leveled the Japanese cities contained at least some nuclear material originally destined for Japan's own atomic program and perhaps for attacks on the United States. Others who have researched the missing uranium believe it may have gone to the Manhattan Project, but not in time to be utilized in the atomic bombs dropped on Japan.

U-234 left Kristiansand, Norway on 15 April 1945, with a conviction among its crew that it would never reach Japan. The commanding officer told the crew that although they were officially destined for Japan, he was firmly convinced in his own mind that their destination would never be reached. With a 75% loss rate among Axis shipping attempting the Germany-Japan trek, the *U-234* captain's feelings were justified.

U-234 slowly made its way across the Atlantic, surfacing only for about two hours each night. She had orders not to jeopardize the mission by attacking other ships. On 4 May, she got a fragmentary message repeated by English and American stations about Admiral Karl Doenitz's elevation to supreme command in Germany. Adolf Hitler was dead. *U-234* was finally forced to surface in order to receive complete signals.

On 10 May, *U-234* picked up the order for all U-boats to surrender and to proceed to an Allied port depending on their position at that time. The U-boat's position determined that it was supposed to surrender to Canada. A heated discussion among the officers and crew ensued over which country should take their surrender. Both the United States and England were considered but the two Japanese officers escorting the cargo desired to go to neither place.

When it became apparent to the Japanese officers that the U-boat commander intended to surrender, they committed suicide and were buried at sea on 11 May.

On 14 May, *U-234* was contacted by the U.S.S. *Sutton* and the German crew surrendered. During the takeover and confiscation of all small arms on board, an American sailor was accidentally shot by another member of the boarding party. He was transferred to the U.S.S. *Forsyth*, along with *U-234*'s medical officer, who assisted during the emergency surgery on the sailor. Although the wounded seaman was stabilized and later transferred to a U.S. Navy hospital, he died a week later from internal bleeding.

The *U-234*'s 41 crew members, six officers and nine passengers were transferred to a U.S. Coast

Guard vessel at sea. The American crew on the German submarine redirected it to the naval shipyard at Portsmouth, New Hampshire, where three other U-boats had already surrendered.

The *U-234*, now flying the Stars and Stripes, is towed into port after its surrender

Among the cargo of the *U-234* was:
- one ton of diplomatic and personal mail
- technical drawings and blueprints for advanced combat weaponry
- plans for construction of jet aircraft factories

- anti-tank weapons and antiaircraft shells
- advanced bombsights and fire-control systems
- airborne radar
- an Me 262 jet fighter, the only jet fighter in existence at the time
- additional jet engines
- 560 kilograms of uranium oxide

The military and civilian experts taken into American custody were:

- Luftwaffe General Ulrich Kessler, on his way to become German air attaché in Tokyo. Kessler's name had been revealed as part of the conspiracy to assassinate Adolf Hitler and he was looking for a way to slip out of the country. The Japanese assignment was the ideal way to disassociate him from the plot.
- Luftwaffe Lieutenant Colonel Fritz von Sandrart and Lieutenant Erich Menzel, experts in air communications, airborne radar, and antiair-craft defenses
- Four Kriegsmarine [Navy] officers, including a naval aviation expert, an antiaircraft expert, a naval construction engineer, and a naval judge tasked with eliminating a huge spy ring funneling information to the Soviets
- August Brinewald and Franz Ruf, experts in the technology and construction of jet aircraft. Their mission was to begin production of jet fighters in Japan
- Dr. Heinz Schlike, a specialist in radar and infrared technologies

Nothing in the *U-234* cargo was more surprising than ten containers filled with 1,200 pounds of uranium oxide, a basic material of atomic bombs. Up to then, the Allies suspected that both Nazi Germany and Japan had nuclear programs but considered them rudimentary and isolated.

Second Officer (Lieutenant) Karl Ernst Pfaff was taken to what he believed to be a top-secret Navy installation in Virginia for interrogation and into a room in which *U-234*'s cargo was being stored. There he was ordered to oversee the opening of a metal container.

The military watchdogs stood back, while a reluctant American with a cutting torch pleaded with Pfaff. "He begged me not to let both of us get blown up, and I assured him that I too did not want to die young. Why would these boxes be booby-trapped? They were on their way to our ally Japan. Why would we want to blow them up?"

When the container had been opened and they saw that it was safe, other military authorities came out of hiding. Pfaff was then asked to open the little cigar box-shaped containers that held the uranium oxide.

The only civilian in the room supervised the operation. "Who is that?" Pfaff asked. "Oppenheimer," somebody said. The name meant nothing to Pfaff. Later, when Pfaff was in Camp Ruston, he read news reports about physicist J. Robert Oppenheimer, director of the Los Alamos laboratory where the design and building of the first atomic bomb had been carried out.

Historians have quietly puzzled over the uranium shipment for years, wondering what the U.S. military did with it. Little headway was made because of restricted access to classified military documents.

The fantastic theory that the uranium was used in the bombs the United States dropped on Hiroshima and Nagasaki, forcing Japan to surrender, is possible but unproven. Key to this theory is the unanswered question of whether the three months between the *U-234's* surrender in May 1945 and the dropping of the U.S. bombs in August 1945 left the Manhattan Project's scientists enough time to incorporate the captured uranium into the Hiroshima and Nagasaki devices.

At least a dozen historians, journalists and nuclear experts around the world have explored the mysteries surrounding the *U-234,* going through newly declassified documents and interviewing aging former members of the German and Japanese militaries and participants in the Manhattan Project.

That the uranium would have been useful to the American atomic bomb effort is certain. "There's no question they were hurting for uranium," Stanley Goldberg, a science historian in Washington who is writing a book on the Manhattan Project, said of the U.S. bomb venture. "They scraped the bottom of the barrel. They came to within an inch of not having enough material for a uranium bomb."

The U-boat's manifest notes the uranium came in ten cases, weighed 560 kilograms and was transported from Germany as an oxide, which is a handy industrial form refined from raw uranium ore. Scientists have determined that amount of uranium oxide would have contained about 3.5 kilograms of the isotope U-235, which is the critical one for making bombs. That amount would have been about a fifth of the total U-235 needed to make one bomb.

John Lansdale displayed no doubts in an interview about the fate of the *U-234's* shipment. "It went to the Manhattan District," he said without hesitation. "It certainly went into the Manhattan District supply of uranium."

Vilma Hunt, a nuclear expert working on a book about uranium used in the war, has researched the fate of the *U-234's* shipment for years. She said she had concluded that it went into the Manhattan Project's mix, not based on any positive evidence she discovered but simply because of the project's great need for weapons material.

"At that time there was a limited amount of uranium oxide available," she said in an interview. "We needed it."

Based on the comments of Lansdale, she added: "You could go as far as saying it was in the stream and would have had a high likelihood that it went into one of the first three bombs. That would have been pushing the system, but that's what they were doing."

The world's first atomic bomb was detonated in the New Mexico desert on 16 July 1945, as a test. Hiroshima was bombed on August 6 and Nagasaki on August 9.

The paper trail seems to indicate the uranium was offloaded from the *U-234* in May but was most likely first shipped to Brooklyn and was still there in July, making it unlikely it was used in the first atomic bombs.

U-234's cargo and passengers were of great value in assessing the state of Japanese technology and defenses for the planned invasion of the Home Islands and in the ensuing Cold War years. Several of the German experts made a swift transition from  POW status to military and industrial employees in the U.S. Prototypes and blueprints hastened development and improvement of many critical American weapons systems, including jet aircraft and ballistic missiles.

By the time Pfaff had completed his work unloading the *U-234*, his shipmates had been scattered among POW camps across the U.S. He was the only member of the *U-234* crew to be sent to Camp Ruston. The aircraft experts Bringewald and Ruf were initially assigned to go to Camp Ruston but the military requested they provide technical assistance at Wright Field in Dayton, Ohio where aircraft research was being conducted. Pfaff's assignment to Camp Ruston was most likely due to the camp's anti-Nazi designation and his cooperation with the U.S. in handling the U-boat's cargo.

U-234 is blown up after its capture

CAMP LIFE

Sports and physical activity was a major pastime among the prisoners. The isolated *U-505* crew engaged in two hours of calisthenics every morning. For the other prisoners, who had access to the athletic field, soccer was the most popular sport.

Sports allowed interaction between the camp's captives and its guards as well as the local citizenry. In 1944, Ruston High School's undefeated football team scrimmaged before the curious POWs who then gave a soccer exhibition in return. Sixty years later, Charles Gullatt still remembered the school's visit to the camp.

"The prisoners displayed their crafts and artwork," Gullatt recalled. "Paintings and things they had made. One prisoner had made a violin out of matchsticks." While the students did not enter the actual prisoner compounds, Gullatt recalled they toured the camp and interacted with the POWs. "We talked with them," Gullatt said. "Many knew English."

The military police guards also played softball matches for POW audiences which led to a request for balls and bats by the prisoners. These activities indicate an amicable if not congenial relationship between the prisoners and their captors. It was not unusual for children of civilian workers at the camp to play games with the prisoners.

Academic pursuits were also popular among the prisoners. American staff and qualified prisoners taught classes which included chemistry, geography, literature, mathematics, and political theory. English classes were provided by American personnel. Heinz Lettau, a German Luftwaffe [Air Force] major, taught a course on meteorology. After the war, he would work for the U.S. military and become one of America's preeminent meteorologists.

The POWs could take college courses as well and enrolled in correspondence study through several American universities. Some colleges provided the courses for free. Lettau recalled in an interview that one university insisting in charging the POWs "out of state tuition."

Prison camp life was not all fun and games. Chores around the compound were mandatory and photographs of the camp indicate it was kept immaculately clean with some attempts at landscaping. Enlisted prisoners worked in maintenance shops, the guard's mess hall, the hospital, and laundry. Many prisoners were loaned out to local farmers. Even the *U-505* crew, after their secret was revealed, worked cotton fields and cut timber throughout the area.

Work details were frequently sent out to other government facilities such as Barksdale Field. Stories abound about the sense of camaraderie that apparently existed between some guards and prisoners. One prisoner asked an American sergeant to help him get his watch repaired. When the sergeant went home to New Jersey on leave, he had the watch repaired at no cost to the prisoner. Other prisoners would count guards among their best friends.

A number of accounts exist of POWs holding a guard's rifle while he completed some chore. Hospital technician Eulis Carroll occasionally drove work crews to Barksdale and usually stopped along the way at a "beer joint" to buy a bottle for each of the POWs in the truck. Before going inside for the beer, Carroll would take off his pistol and leave it in the truck, fully accessible to the prisoners.

Each compound of the camp was serviced by a canteen where prisoners could buy toiletries and other items. The canteens were operated by a staff of prisoners supervised by the Camp's Post Exchange officer. Among the most commonly sold items were pens, pencils, notebooks, magazines, newspapers, paperback books, tobacco products, and playing cards. Until mid-1945, a number of food and refreshment items were available for purchase by the prisoners. Prisoners could buy candy, chewing gum, cookies, soft drinks, and up to two bottles of '3.2' beer.

In the mess halls, prisoners ate as well as their keepers, possibly even better, since the prisoners at Ruston had some excellent cooks among their numbers. Some foodstuffs in short supply among the

German cooks (in white) in mess hall with American guards

civilian populace could be found in the camp's kitchens. Across the nation, however, public pressure was brought to alter prisoner meals so that they did not appear to be serving their time in luxury accommodations. In May 1945, the Provost Marshal

General, supervisor of all POW camps, restricted foods available to prisoners and prohibited further sale of candy, cookies, beer and soft drinks.

Some of the prisoners passed the time creating intricate crafts. In front of many barracks were miniature models created of rocks, cement and mud. In front of one barrack in the Afrika Korps compound was a sports complex about ten feet square containing a soccer field, racetrack, tennis courts and other facilities. Other barracks boasted five-foot high Bavarian castles, fountains, and busts of Frederick the Great, all made of scrap materials picked up around the camp.

One of the elaborate castles German prisoners constructed outside a barracks at Camp Ruston

Music was an important aspect of camp life. The prisoners had their own orchestra. Radio station KDKH in Shreveport even broadcast a musical production of the Ruston POWs consisting of a medley of waltzes, foxtrots, and jazz songs.

Movies were shown regularly to the prisoners but no motion picture had the impact of film of the German concentration camps, gas chambers, and mass graves. Horst Blumenberg recalled the disturbing films in a 2000 interview:

"We went to our monthly movie show and nothing happened. They had the lights already turned off, [but] nothing happened. Suddenly, all the emergency exits opened, about 200 MPs pile in, armed to the teeth. What now? Suddenly, they show the Holocaust movies."

The POWs were visibly shaken by the images, staring in disbelief that their government would commit such atrocities. It was one thing to kill in battle, another to be a murderer. "We weren't even in Germany when it all happened," Blumenberg recalled. "We didn't even know about it."

Not all the prisoners at Camp Ruston were career soldiers. Many were professionals who found themselves in the military in a time of war. Their ranks included professional painters and other artists, musicians, physicians, and university professors. By practicing their trades at Camp Ruston, they helped their fellow inmates through the tedious days behind the barbed wire, half a world from home.

Another castle in the immaculate prisoner's compound

ESCAPES

Although the internees of Camp Ruston were well treated and did not want for necessities or even conveniences, prisoners in a time of war are expected to attempt to escape their captors. Every soldier occupied with guarding prisoners is one less soldier engaged in the fight. The *U-505* crew was probably more serious about this obligation than other occupants of the camp.

Camp Ruston experienced several escapes but most of the prisoners were recaptured within twenty-four hours. Escapes were rare and usually involved men walking off from work details outside the camp. Most escapees were just looking for a little time away from the camp. Only 34 prisoners went over the wire and eluded capture for more than 24 hours. It was not unusual for an escapee to turn himself in or return to the camp when he got hungry. There is no record that any escapee ever committed a crime while outside the camp, another indication that most escapes were simply adventures into the countryside rather than serious efforts to evade capture.

The *U-505* crew engaged in the most intensive effort to escape by working on tunnels to reach the outer wire fence enclosing the camp. Otto Dietz recalled one tunnel in an interview during one of his return visits to Camp Ruston after the war:

"After we dug for about three to four weeks, day and night, it was discovered. Although we were very careful, putting the earth on the ceiling boards [of the barracks], it finally happened. The Red Cross was to visit the camp. For reasons of secrecy, we were all [taken] to Camp Livingston for several days. When we returned, the tunnel was gone."

FBI wanted poster for prisoner Charly King, the only escapee to elude capture

The records appear to show only one POW successfully escaped Camp Ruston and made his way to freedom. Charley King was born in Panama, the parents of a Texas-born mother. His father was a naturalized American citizen. In 1929, he and his family moved to Germany and became German citizens. King was again living in Panama when war broke out. He returned to Germany in 1941 and was inducted into the army. After a failed escape attempt in March 1945, King indicated his plan had been to

41

proceed west to Texas and then to Mexico and on to Panama, using his fluency in English, Spanish, and German to his advantage. There is no evidence that King was ever apprehended and he is the only prisoner known to have eluded capture.

The only U-boat sailor known to have escaped Camp Ruston was Horst Blumenberg of the *U-664*. Blumenberg escaped several times for short periods of time. In July 1945, the young sailor and three other prisoners escaped from the branch camp at Barksdale Army Airfield. Guards shot at them as they made their way to the Red River where they found a log and floated away. They lived off the land for about a week before their recapture and return to Camp Ruston where they were placed in isolation. Blumenberg once described another escape in which he went over the camp's wire fence but was apprehended by a local law officer who fed him a hamburger and Coke before returning him to the camp. To Blumenberg, the thrill of the escape, even for a short respite outside the wire, was worth any punishment the authorities could impose.

There is no record that any of the *U-505* sailors ever escaped, even temporarily, despite their tunneling efforts.

WAR'S END

After Japan's surrender in September 1945, Camp Ruston acted as a center for repatriation of prisoners out of the United States. On 3 February 1946, the last prisoners left Camp Ruston, and the Camp was officially closed on 5 June 1946.

Over time, the buildings of Camp Ruston came down. In 1946, the property was deeded to the State of Louisiana so the huge hospital could be used as a tuberculosis sanitarium. Inmates from the state penitentiary at Angola were used to tear down many of the buildings.

Despite the end of the war, the *U-505* crew was still years from home. The sailors finally saw  Germany again after spending several years in British labor camps. Some of the sailors, including Hans Goebeler, returned to Ruston over the next fifty years to visit the former Camp. In a 1984 visit, Goebeler, who would always be known as the sailor who "plugged the plug" on the *U-505,* described his experience in the POW Camp. "After three years on a sub," he reminisced, "life at Camp Ruston was like a vacation."

Like Goebeler, Horst Blumenberg had to return to Germany by way of a European labor camp. The labor camps were unlike the comforts of Camp Ruston. "You can understand being behind the barbed wire during wartime," Blumenberg said in an interview, "but if there is another year going by and another year going by, then it gets pretty annoying."

A number of former Camp Ruston prisoners eventually immigrated to the United States, including Goebeler, Blumenberg, and Ernst Pfaff. Blumenberg left Camp Ruston with the intentions of returning to America as soon as possible.

"The day I walked through the door [in returning home in 1947]," Blumenberg said, "my mother asked me, 'What are you going to do?' I say, the first chance I have, I'm going back to America. She said, 'You haven't even sat down yet after all those years and you're telling me you will go to America?' I said yes. Which I did." Blumenberg moved to the United

States in the 1950's and worked as an engineer and retired in Kentucky.

Numerous former prisoners made return visits to Camp Ruston, usually igniting renewed interest in the camp. Horst Blumenberg made his first visit back to the camp in 1966 and in late 2004, declared he intended to make another visit soon.

Hans Goebeler died in 1999. His family still runs the company he started, selling mugs and t-shirts adorned with the photos of famous U-boat commanders and other military leaders.

Pfaff was held at Camp Ruston and other POW camps until early 1946 when he returned to Germany and married and prepared for a brighter future.

"I had taken a liking to this country and to the American style," Pfaff said, and he immediately began planning his strategy to return to the United States.

Denim work jacket from Louisiana Tech's Camp Ruston Collection. While prisoners could wear their uniforms, they usually did not do so on work details. All work clothes were stenciled with "PW" on the back and sleeves.

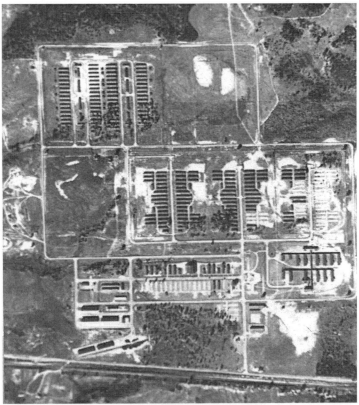
Camp Ruston in 1947 after some buildings had been demolished

He found his way to Montreal in 1951, and lived there nineteen years, working for the Caterpillar Company. He lived in Memphis for another nineteen years, and finally retired to Bellingham, Washington in 1991.

"The war was a different part of my life," Pfaff said in an interview, "something people don't understand. When the war was over and we had lost it, I had to do something and start another part of my life. I disappeared from the surface. Nobody, except my close friend Fehler (commander of the *U-234*), knew where I was."

Today a state facility for the mentally disabled encompasses a few acres of the once gigantic camp. A large portion is now pastureland owned by Louisiana Tech University. Like most World War II POW Camps in the U.S., little remains today to mark the ground once inhabited by thousands of soldiers and sailors. Only two dilapidated buildings remain but the rough outline of the compounds can still be seen.

∧   ∧   ∧

Life as a U-boat submariner during World War II was an undescribable adventure. The fear, the dangers, and the very nature of life underwater required a strength of character and nerve beyond comprehension. Duty on a U-boat was dangerous. Germany sent 859 U-boats out on war patrols; 648 were lost at sea. Over 400 of these yielded no survivors. So compared to the potential consequences, life at Camp Ruston drew few complaints.

Numerous former prisoners called life at Camp Ruston "like a vacation," but Horst Blumenberg noted life anywhere on shore can not compare to the tough life of a submariner. Cramped in an iron tomb, breathing squalid air perfumed by the sweat of other men, the crew of a U-boat knew the likelihood of seeing Germany again was impossible to calculate.

Like America as a whole, the community of Ruston fervently supported its troops and the war effort. The Germans and Japanese were viewed as evil and less than human. Government propaganda did nothing to dispute this image.

Camp Ruston put a different face on the enemy. Ruth Futrell recalled seeing POWs arrive on the train and was surprised that they were "young boys with sweet faces." They waved and smiled as they passed the Ruston depot on the way to the camp. They reminded people of their own young men overseas.

Mary Duchaney had some of the closest contact with the prisoners as she worked in the camp hospital. In an interview, she said, "We can be proud of the fact that we took soldiers who fought our boys and possibly killed some of them and treated them humanely...we treated them with kindness and consideration for the most part." Duchaney readily admitted her attitude towards the enemy changed because of her interaction with Camp Ruston POWs.

For the prisoners, Camp Ruston revealed the United States as a land of vast resources and opportunities. Their capture altered their lives by opening their eyes to what America had to offer. Once they had a glimpse of American life, many could not resist the temptation.

For soldiers, prisoners, and local citizens, association with Camp Ruston was an unforgettable experience that molded their future attitudes towards their fellow man.

U-505 sailors working cotton fields near Ruston

APPENDIX

The Appendix contains the following U.S. Navy documents:

U.S. Navy Department press release
on the capture of *U-505*

U.S. Naval Historical Center paper,
"Capture of the *U-505*."

Medal of Honor Citation
for Lieutenant (j.g.) Albert David

NAVY DEPARTMENT
MAY 16, 1945

IMMEDIATE RELEASE
PRESS AND RADIO

CAPTURE OF NAZI SUBMARINE IN NINTEEN FORTY-FOUR REVEALED

One of the best kept secrets of the war was revealed today by announcement that on June 4, 1944, a U.S. Navy escort carrier task group reverted to the tactics of the early Continental Navy and hunted down, attacked, boarded, and captured the Nazi submarine U-505, 150 miles west of Cape Blanco in French West Africa. The Task Group then towed their prize 2,500 miles to Naval Operating Base, Bermuda. This was the first time the U.S. Navy had boarded and captured a foreign enemy man-of-war in battle on the high seas since 1815.

The Task Group consisted of the baby flattop U.S.S. GUADALCANAL and her five destroyer escorts. The group was commanded by Captain Daniel V. Gallery, U.S.N., a veteran Naval Aviator of 1256 McAllister Place, Chicago, Illinois, and Vienna, Virginia, who was also Commanding Officer of the GUADALCANAL.

Other units of the Task Group were the U.S.S. PILLSBURY, commanded by Lieutenant Commander George W. Cassleman, U.S.N.R., of 1020 Barthelme Street, Joliet, Illinois; U.S.S. CHATELAIN, under command of Lieutenant Commander Dudley S. Knox, U.S.N.R., of 1512 34th Street, Northwest, Washington, D.C.; U.S.S. POPE, under Lieutenant Commander Edwin H. Headland, Jr., U.S.N., of Henriette, Minnesota; U.S.S. FLAHERTY, under Lieutenant Commander Means Johnston, Jr., U.S.N., of Greenwood, Mississippi, and U.S.S. JENKS, under Lieutenant Commander, Julius F. Way, U.S.N., of Stonington, Maine. Commander Frederick S. Hall, U.S.N., of 16 Elm Avenue, Wyoming, Ohio, was the destroyer division commander and Lieutenant Norman D. Hodson, U.S.N., of 1508 G. Street, San Bernardino, California, commanded the GUADAL-CANAL's aircraft squadron.

The capture occurred while the U-505 was returning to her base after an 80-day commerce destroying raid in the Gulf of Guinea. The U-boat was running completely submerged and was in perfect position to attack the GUADALCANAL when first detected by the sound gear of the CHATELAIN in the GUADALCANAL's screen. Fighter planes from the carrier spotted the deep running sub from the air and guided the destroyers to the attack by firing their fixed guns into the water and zooming the spot directly over the submerged sub. Following directions given from the air by two fighter pilots from Composite Squadron Eight, flying from the GUADALCANAL, Lieutenant Wolffe W. Roberts, U.S.N.R., of 611 10th Avenue, Lewiston, Idaho, and Lieutenant John W. Cadle, Jr., U.S.N.R., of 212 Ottawa Avenue, Dixon, Illinois, the CHATELAIN delivered a damaging depth charge attack which forced the U-boat to the surface right in the middle of the task group.

The task group immediately deluged the cornered U-boat with fire from small caliber automatic weapons. In accordance with previously laid plans for

51

driving the crew overboard without doing serious structural damage to the sub, only anti-personnel ammunition was fired instead of the usual armor piercing shells. The Nazis tried to man their guns and fight it out on the surface but they were soon driven overboard by the hail of machine gun bullets from the task group. They left their U-boat circling at speed on the surface, and rapidly filling with water through the scuttling valves which they opened when they abandoned ship.

All ships of the task group dropped whale boats in the water with trained boarding parties as soon as the Nazis began abandoning ship. These boats raced after the circling submarine, while the GUADAL-CANAL dodged the one torpedo which the Nazis were able to fire before leaving their ship.

The PILLSBURY's whale boat, commanded by Lieutenant Albert L. David, U.S.N., of 4175 36th Street, San Diego, California, was the first to get alongside the runaway submarine. Lieutenant David, who was Assistant Engineering and Electrical Officer of the PILLSBURY, and eight enlisted men from the PILLSBURY leaped aboard the submarine and plunged down the conning tower hatch with tommy guns and hand grenades to fight it out with any Nazis left on board. They found only one dead man. This boarding party was soon reinforced by a larger party from the GUADALCANAL under the command of Commander Earl Trosino, U.S.N.R., of 241 Sunny-brook Road, Springfield, Pennsylvania.

The boarding parties performed numerous heroic and remarkable acts in preventing their damaged prize from sinking. They took over the U-boat in a foundering condition, with water pouring into the hull in many places. Most of the boarders had never set foot on a submarine before, but despite the danger of

booby traps, and working against time, which was rapidly running out, the boarding parties plugged all leaks, found and closed the scuttling valves. The flooding was checked just in time to prevent the U-boat from plunging to the bottom, and taking the boarding parties with her. To prevent the seas from washing down the conning tower hatch as the sub sank in the water, it had been necessary to close the hatch behind the boarding parties, thus barring their only avenue of escape in case the U-boat foundered.

Captain Gallery, who is an ordnance expert as well as a flyer, boarded the sub and opened a suspected booby trap on the water tight door to the after torpedo room, to enable the salvage parties to stop the flooding in that part of the sub.

The original boarding party from the PILLSBURY consisted of the following men in addition to Lieutenant David:

Arthur William Knispel, Torpedoman, Second Class, U.S.N.R., 344-1/2 South 12th Street, Newark, New Jersey.

Stanley Edward Wdowiak, Radioman, Second Class, U.S.N.R., 124 Maeserale, Brooklyn, New York.

Chester Anthony Mocarski, Gunner's Mate, First Class, U.S.N.R., 7706 Star Avenue, Brooklyn, New York.

Wayne McVeigh Pickles, Jr., Boatswain's Mate, Second Class, U.S.N., 647 Wheaton Road, San Antonio, Texas.

George William Jacobson, Chief Motor Machinist's Mate, U.S.N.R., 7234 North Wabash Avenue, Portland, Oregon.

Zenon Benedict Lukosius, Motor Machinist's Mate, First Class, U.S.N., of 14105 South Edbrooke Avenue, Riverdale, Illinois, whose mother, Mrs. Barbera Wngalis, lives at 128 East 104th Place, Chicago, Illinois.

William Roland Riendeau, Electrician's Mate, Second Class, U.S.N., 1157 North Main Street, Providence, Rhode Island.

Gordan Fritz Hohne, Signalman, Second Class, U.S.N.R., of 28 Marconi Road, Worchester, Massachusetts.

The crew of the PILLSBURY's whale boat were:

Philip Norman Trusheim, Coxswain, U.S.N., of Costa Mesa, California.

Robert Rosco Jenkins, Motor Maschinist's Mate, Third Class, U.S.N.R., of Gypsy, West Virginia.

James Ernest Beaver, Jr., Seaman, First Class, U.S.N.R., of 22 Ohio Street, Atco, Georgia.

After flooding had been stopped the U-boat was taken in tow by the GUADALCANAL. Because the task group was in submarine infested waters the GUADALCANAL maintained continuous air patrols, conducting flight operations day and night with her prize in tow. The Fleet Tug ABNAKI, was rushed to the scene by orders from Admiral R.S. Ingersoll, U.S.N., Commander in Chief, Atlantic Fleet, and relieved the GUADALCANAL of the towing job four days after the capture.

American sailors on the U-505 with the carrier U.S.S. Guadalcanal in the background

Among the many amazing and ingenious feats performed by the salvage parties was that of recharging the submarine's batteries. Commander Trosino disconnected the sub's diesels from her motors in order to allow the propellers to turn the shafts when the sub was being towed. Ensign Fred Middaugh, of Los Angles, California, traced out the sub's electric wiring and set the main switches for charging the batteries. The GUADALCANAL then towed the U-505 at high speed, thus turning the electric motors over, causing them to operate as generators and to recharge the batteries. This enabled the salvage parties to run all the electric machinery in the boat and to use her own pumps and air compressors to bring her up to full surface trim.

The ABNAKI, escorted by the task group, towed the U-boat 2,500 miles to the U.S. Naval Operating Base, Bermuda, where she was turned over to experts from the Office of Naval Intelligence flown out from Washington. The technical and operational information obtained as a result of the capture are said to have played an important part in clinching the Battle of the Atlantic and thus shortening the war by some months. The U-505 is now in the service of the Navy, manned by a U.S. Naval crew, in the category of a captured enemy vessel.

Fifty-eight survivors (including the captain) from the U-505's crew of 59 were rescued and imprisoned in the United States.

The only other German submarine ever captured at sea in this war or in World War No. 1, was a Nazi U-boat which was beached on the south coast of Iceland in 1941, after her surrender. This U-boat was

U-505 **Commander Lange is transferred to the U.S.S. Guadalcanal for medical treatment**

crippled by an RAF plane and surrendered to a British trawler in a storm several hundred miles south of Iceland. The crew of this U-boat cooperated with the British in towing the submarine to the spot where she was beached after the surrender. They were in full control of the U-boat while she was being towed and were able to destroy nearly all material which had any intelligence value. The U-505 was taken intact, just as her crew had left her, believing that they had scuttled her in accordance with standard practice.

Captain Gallery says, "I consider this capture to be proof for posterity of the versatility and courage of the present day American sailor. All ships in this task group were less than a year old and 80 percent of the officers and men were serving in their first seagoing ship. All hands did their stuff like veteran sea dogs, and airplane mechanics became submarine experts in a hurry, when the chips were down. I'm sure John Paul Jones and his men were proud of these lads and of the day's work when the U.S. colors went up on the U-505."

Admiral R.E. Ingersoll, U.S.N., Commander in Chief, U.S. Atlantic Fleet, cited the Task Group as follows:

"For outstanding performance during anti-submarine operations in the eastern Atlantic on June 4, 1944, when the Task Group attacked, boarded and captured the German Submarine U-505.

"Setting out on an anti-submarine sweep with the stated purpose of capturing and bringing back to the United States a German submarine, all units of the

Task Group worked incessantly throughout the cruise to prepare themselves for the accomplishment of this exceedingly difficult purpose. Locating a single U-boat after a long period of fruitless searches, the entire Task Group participated in further intensive search and hold down operations which terminated in the sighting of the submerged submarine by an airplane. An extremely accurate initial depth charge attack by the U.S.S. CHATELAIN forced the U-boat to the surface where it was subjected to the combined automatic weapons fire of three destroyer escorts and two aircraft. This anti-personnel attack completely achieved its pre-conceived objective in forcing the entire enemy crew to abandon ship while inflicting relatively minor material damage on the submarine.

"Completely unmindful of the dangers involved all units of the Task Group then proceeded to carry out their assigned duties in accomplishing the actual capture. The U.S.S. PILLSBURY, badly damaged in a series of attempts to go alongside the erratically maneuvering submarine in order to transfer a mass boarding and repair party, was forced to withdraw and to transfer necessary personnel by small boat. Undeterred by the apparent sinking condition of the U-boat, the danger of explosions of demolition and scuttling charges, and the probability of enemy gunfire, the small boarding party plunged through the conning tower hatch, did everything in its power to keep the submarine afloat and removed valuable papers and documents. Succeeding, and more fully equipped, salvage parties, faced with dangers similar to those which confronted the first group to enter the submarine, performed seemingly impossible tasks in keeping the U-boat afloat until it could be taken in tow by the U.S.S. GUADALCANAL. After three days of ceaseless labor the captured U-boat was seaworthy and able to withstand, with constant care, the vigors of a twenty-four hundred mile tow to its destination.

"The Task Group's brilliant achievement in disabling, capturing, and towing to a United States base a modern enemy man-of-war taken in combat on the high seas is a feat unprecedented in individual and group bravery, execution, and accomplishment in the Naval History of the United States."

Lieutenant David was awarded a Navy Cross for his part in the episode, Captain Gallery, for his services in the Atlantic anti-submarine warfare, was awarded a Distinguished Service Medal.

(Photographs available in Photographic Library, Office of Public Relations.)

***

CAPTURE OF THE U-505

U.S. Naval Historical Center
805 Kidder Breese St. SE
Washington Navy Yard, DC 20374-5060

On 4 June 1944, a hunter-killer group of the United States Navy captured the German submarine *U-505*. This event marked the first time a U.S. Navy vessel had captured an enemy vessel at sea since the nineteenth century. The action took place in the Atlantic Ocean, in Latitude 21-30N, Longitude 19-20W, about 150 miles off the coast of Rio De Oro, Africa. The American force was commanded by Captain Daniel V. Gallery, USN, and comprised the escort Carrier *Guadalcanal* (CVE-60) and five escort vessels under Commander Frederick S. Hall, USN: *Pillsbury* (DE-133) *Pope* DE-134), *Flaherty* (DE-135), *Chatelain* (DE-149), and *Jenks* (DE-665).

Alerted by American cryptanalysts, who--along with the British--had been decrypting the German naval code, the *Guadalcanal* task group knew U-boats were operating off the African coast near Cape Verde. They did not know the precise location, however, because the exact coordinates (latitude and longitude) in the message were encoded separately before being enciphered for transmission. By adding this regional information together with high-frequency direction finding fixes (HF/DF)--which tracked U-boats by radio transmissions--and air and surface recon-naissance, the Allies could narrow down a U-boat's location to a small area. The *Guadalcanal* task group intended to use all these methods to find and capture the next U-boat they encountered through the use of trained boarding parties.

The task group sailed from Norfolk, Virginia, on 15 May 1944 for an anti-submarine patrol near the Canary Islands. For two weeks they searched unsuccessfully, even steaming as far south as Freetown, Sierra Leone, in a vain effort to locate a U-boat. On Sunday, 4 June 1944, with fuel running low, the warships' reluctantly turned north and headed for Casablanca. Ironically, not ten minutes later at 1109 that morning, U.S.S. *Chatelain* (DE-149), Lieutenant Commander Dudley S. Knox, USNR, made sonar contact on an object just 800 yards away on her starboard bow. *Guadalcanal* immediately swung clear at top speed, desperately trying to avoid getting in the way, as *Chatelain* and the other escorts closed the position.

In the minutes required to identify the contact definitely as a submarine, however, *Chatelain* closed too rapidly and could not attack—as her depth charges would not sink fast enough to intercept the U-boat. The escort held her fire instead, opened range and setup a deliberate attack with her "hedgehog" (ahead-thrown depth charges which explode on contact only) battery. Regaining sonar contact after a momentary loss due to the short range, *Chatelain* passed beyond the submarine and swung around toward it to make a second attack with depth charges.

As the ship heeled over in her tight turn, one of two General Motors FM-2 "Wildcat" fighter planes launched overhead by *Guadalcanal*, sighted the submerged U-boat and dived on it, firing into the water to mark the submarine's position. *Chatelain* steadied up on her sound bearing and moved in for the kill. A full pattern of depth charges set for a shallow target splashed into the water around the U-boat. As their detonations threw geysers of spray into

The *U-505* under depth charge attack by two U.S. destroyers

the air, a large oil slick spread on the water; the fighter plane overhead radioed "You struck oil! Sub is surfacing!" Just six and one-half minutes after *Chatelain's* first attack, *U-505* broke the surface with its rudder jammed, lights and electrical machinery out, and water coming in.

As the submarine broached only 700 yards from *Chatelain*, the escort opened fire with all automatic weapons that would bear and swept the U-boat's decks. *Pillsbury*, Lieutenant George W. Casselman, USNR, and *Jenks*, Lieutenant Commander Julius F. Way, USN, farther away, and the two "Wildcats" overhead all joined the shooting and added to the intense barrage. Wounded in the torrent of fire and believing that his submarine had been mortally damaged by *Chatelain's* depth charges, the commanding officer of *U-505* quickly ordered his crew to abandon ship. So quickly was this command obeyed that scuttling measures were left incomplete and the submarine's engines continued to run.

The jammed rudder caused the partially-submerged *U-505* to circle to the right at a speed near seven knots. Seeing the U-boat turning toward him, the commanding officer of *Chatelain* ordered a single torpedo fired at the submarine in order to forestall what appeared to be a similar attack on himself. The torpedo passed ahead of *U-505*, which by now appeared to be completely abandoned. About two minutes later, the escort division commander ordered cease fire and called away *Pillsbury's* boarding party.

While *Chatelain* and *Jenks* picked up survivors, *Pillsbury* sent its motor whaleboat to the circling submarine where Lieutenant (junior grade) Albert L. David, USN, led the eight-man party on board. Despite the probability of *U-505* sinking or blowing up at any minute and not knowing what form of resistance they might meet below, David and his men clambered up the conning tower and then down the hatches into the boat itself. After a quick examination proved the U-boat was completely deserted (except for one dead man on deck—the only fatality of the action), the boarders set about bundling up charts, code books, and papers, disconnecting demolition charges, closing valves, and plugging leaks. By the time the flood of water had been stopped, the U-boat was low in the water and down by the stern.

Part of the boarding party that captured the *U-505*

Dazed prisoners from the *U-505*

Meanwhile, *Pillsbury* twice went alongside the turning submarine to put over tow lines and each time the escort's side was pierced by the U-boats' bow plane. Finally, with three compartments flooded, she was forced to haul clear to attend to her own damage. The boarding party was then reinforced by a party from *Guadalcanal.* Led by Commander Earl Trosino, USNR, the carrier's men completed temporary salvage measures, and took a towline from the *Guadalcanal.* The salvage crew was later joined by USN Commander Colby G. Rucker, who arrived with the seaplane tender *Humbolt* (AVP-21).

In an ingenious solution to the heavy flooding, the salvage crew disconnected the boat's diesels from her motors. This allowed the propellers to turn the shafts while under tow. After setting the main switches to charge the batteries, *Guadalcanal* towed the U-boat at high speed, turning the electric motors over which recharged the boat's batteries. With power restored, the salvage crew could use the U-boat's own pumps and air compressors to finish pumping out seawater and bring her up to full surface trim.

After three days of towing, *Guadalcanal* was relieved of her burden by the fleet tug *Abnaki* (ATF-96). Arriving with the tug was the tanker *Kennebec* (AO-36), sent to provide much-needed fuel to the hunter-killer group. On Monday, 19 June 1944, *U-505* was brought into Port Royal Bay, Bermuda, after a tow of 1,700 miles.

The *U-505,* already flying the flag of its captors, sinks fast as Lt. (j.g.) David and sailors attempt to salvage it

Fifty-eight prisoners had been taken from the water during the action. One man had been killed and three (505's commanding officer, executive officer, and one enlisted man) wounded. For his part in saving the abandoned submarine, Lieutenant(jg) David was awarded the Medal of Honor; Torpedoman's Mate Third Class A. Knispel and Radioman

Second Class S. E. Wdowiak, each received the Navy Cross; and Commander Trosino received the Legion of Merit.

The task group itself was awarded the Presidential Unit citation, in part because of the unique and difficult feat of boarding and capturing an enemy warship on the high-seas—something the U.S. Navy had not accomplished since the 19th-century. More significantly, however, the capture of codebooks on U-505 allowed American cryptanalysts to occasionally break the special "coordinate" code in enciphered German messages and determine more precise locations for U-boat operating areas. In addition to vectoring in hunter-killer task groups on these locations, these coordinates enabled Allied convoy commanders to route shipping away from known U-boat locations, greatly inhibiting the effectiveness of German submarine patrols.

Admiral Royal E. Ingersoll, Commander in Chief, U.S. Atlantic Fleet, cited the Task Group as follows:

"For outstanding performance during anti-submarine operations in the eastern Atlantic on June 4, 1944, when the Task group attacked, boarded and captured the German submarine U-505."

"Setting out on an anti-submarine sweep with the stated purpose of capturing and bringing back to the United States a German submarine, all units of the Task Group worked incessantly throughout the cruise to prepare themselves for the accomplishment of this exceedingly difficult purpose. Locating a single U-boat after a long period of fruitless searches, the entire Task Group participated in intensive search and hold down operations which terminated in the sighting of the submerged submarine by an airplane. An extremely accurate initial depth charge attack by the U.S.S. *Chatelain* forced the U-boat to surface where it was subjected to the combined automatic weapons fire of three destroyer escorts and two aircraft. This anti-personnel attack completely achieved its pre-conceived objective in forcing the entire enemy crew to abandon ship while inflicting relatively minor material damage on the submarine."

"Completely unmindful of the dangers involved all units of the Task Group then proceeded to carry out their assigned duties in accomplishing the actual capture. The U.S.S. *Pillsbury*, badly damaged in a series of attempts to go alongside the erratically maneuvering submarine in order to transfer a mass boarding and repair party, was forced to withdraw and to transfer necessary personnel by small boat. Undeterred by the apparent sinking condition of the U-boat, the danger of explosions of demolition and scuttling charges, and the probability of enemy gunfire, the small boarding party plunged through the conning tower hatch, did everything in its power to keep the submarine afloat and remove valuable papers and documents. Succeeding, and more fully equipped, salvage parties, faced with dangers similar to those which confronted the first group to enter the submarine, performed seemingly impossible tasks in keeping the U-boat afloat until it could be taken in tow by the U.S.S. *Guadalcanal.* After three days of ceaseless labor the captured U-boat was seaworthy and able to withstand, with constant care, the vigors of a twenty-four hundred mile tow to its destination."

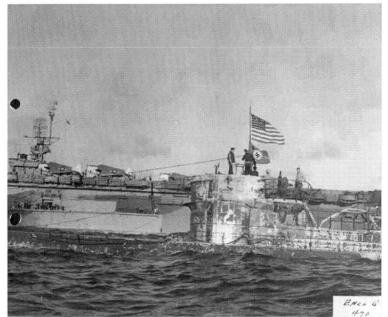

The *U-505,* alongside the U.S.S. *Guadalcanal,* flying both the U.S. and German flags

"The Task Group's brilliant achievement in disabling, capturing, and towing to a United States base a modern enemy man-of-war taken in combat on the high seas is a feat unprecedented in individual and group bravery, execution, and accomplishment in the Naval History of the United States."

Disposition of *U-505*

As the U.S. Navy was far more interested in the advanced engineering design of fast underwater U-boats--such as the streamlined German Type XXI and XXIII submarines--rather than the familiar fleet-boat types illustrated by the *U-505*, the captured submarine was investigated by Navy intelligence and engineering officers during 1945 and then promptly slated for disposal. The intention was to use the hulk for gunnery and torpedo target practice, a fate similar to those of many other captured enemy submarines.

In 1946, however, Father John Gallery learned of this plan from his brother (then Admiral Daniel Gallery) and called the Chicago Museum of Science and Industry (MSI) President Lenox Lohr to see if MSI would have an interest in saving *U-505*. The museum, established by Chicago businessman Julius Rosenwald as a center for "industrial enlightenment" and public science education, specialized in interactive exhibits, not just view displays and artifacts. Lohr immediately revealed 10-year old plans to include a submarine in the exhibits of the museum and began a plan to bring the *U-505* to Chicago.

The people of Chicago raised $250,000 to help prepare the boat for the tow and installation at the museum. In September 1954, *U-505* was donated to Chicago at no cost to the U.S. Government. On September 25, 1954 *U-505* was dedicated as a war memorial and as a permanent exhibit. In 1989, the *U-505*--as the only Type IX-C boat still in existence--was designated a National Historic Landmark.

Select Bibliography

"Capture of Nazi Submarine in 1944 Revealed" Navy Department Press Release, 16 May 1945. [Located in Naval Historical Center, Ships' History Branch, U.S.S. *Flaherty* (DE-135) file].

Hinsley, F. H. et al. *British Intelligence in the Second World War: Its Influence on Strategy and Operations.* vol. 2. New York: Cambridge University Press, 1981. [See p.552 for information on codebooks captured on *U-505*].

Morison, Samuel Eliot. *The Atlantic Battle Won: May 1943-May 1945.* vol. 10 of *History of United States Naval Operations in World War II.* Boston: Little, Brown and Co., 1960. [For a description of the capture see pp. 290-93.

Ratcliff, R. A. "Searching for Security: The German Investigations into Enigma's Security" *Intelligence and National Security* 14, no.1 (Spring 1999): 146-167. [See p.156 for information on codebooks captured on *U-505.*].

MEDAL OF HONOR CITATION
LIEUTENANT (j.g.) ALBERT LEROY DAVID
FOR CAPTURE OF THE U-505

Rank and organization: Lieutenant, Junior Grade, U.S. Navy. Born: 18 July 1902, Maryville, Mo. Accredited to: Missouri. Other Navy award: Navy Cross with gold star.

Citation: For conspicuous gallantry and intrepidity at the risk of his life above and beyond the call of duty while attached to the U.S.S. *Pillsbury* during the capture of an enemy German submarine off French West Africa, 4 June 1944. Taking a vigorous part in the skillfully coordinated attack on the German *U-505* which climaxed a prolonged search by the Task Group, Lt. (then Lt. j.g.) David boldly led a party from the *Pillsbury* in boarding the hostile submarine as it circled erratically at 5 or 6 knots on the surface. Fully aware that the U-boat might momentarily sink or be blown up by exploding demolition and scuttling charges, he braved the added danger of enemy gunfire to plunge through the conning tower hatch and, with his small party, exerted every effort to keep the ship afloat and to assist the succeeding and more fully equipped salvage parties in making the *U-505* seaworthy for the long tow across the Atlantic to a U.S. port. By his valiant service during the first successful boarding and capture of an enemy man-o-war on the high seas by the U.S. Navy since 1815, Lt. David contributed materially to the effectiveness of our Battle of the Atlantic and upheld the highest traditions of the U.S. Naval Service.

REFERENCES

American Stalag. Videotape. A.M. Productions with University of Florida, 2000.

Blair, Clay. *Hitler's U-boat War: The Hunted, 1942-1945.* New York: Random House, 1998.

Broad, William W. "Captured Cargo, Captivating Mystery." *New York Times.* December 31, 1995, 22A.

Camp Ruston Collection. Prescott Memorial Library, Louisiana Tech University.

Duhe, Jeff. *Louisiana Parade I: Camp Ruston German POW Camp.* Louisiana Public Broadcasting, N.d.

Goebeler, Hans and Vanzo, John. *Steel Boats, Iron Hearts: The Wartime Sage of Hans Goebeler and the U-505.* Holder, FL: Wagnerian Publications, 1999.

Hammond, Pat. "Nazi Sub: How U-234 Brought Its Deadly Secret Cargo to New Hampshire." (Manchester) *New Hampshire Sunday News,* April 30, 1995.

Krammer, Arnold. *Nazi Prisoners of War in America.* Lanham, MD: Scarborough House Publishers, 1991.

Miller, David. *U-Boats: The Illustrated History of the Raiders of the Deep.* Dulles, VA: Pegasus Publishing, 2000.

Morden, Bettie J. *The Women's Army Corps, 1945-1978.* Washington, DC: Center for Military History, U.S. Army, 2000.

Otts, Daniel Oscar. *A Historical Study of the Ruston Prisoner of War Camp.* Unpublished thesis for Northeast Louisiana University, Monroe, LA, 1971.

Ruston (La.) *Daily Leader, 1942, 1943, 1946, 1947, 1984.*

Shreveport (La.) *Times, 1983, 1984, 1993.*

Scalia, Joseph Mark. *Germany's Last Mission to Japan: The Failed Voyage of U-234.* Annapolis, MD: Naval Institute Press, 1999.

United States Navy documents and photographs, U.S. Naval Historical Center, Washington, DC.

Wilhelm, Kathy. *"'You're a Soldier:' Branch A of the Fifth Women's Army Auxiliary Corps Training Center, Camp Ruston, Louisiana."* North Louisiana Historical Association Journal. Fall 1997.

Photo credits

Camp Ruston Collection, Prescott Memorial Library, Louisiana Tech University, Ruston, LA: Front cover left, 3, 5, bottom 6, 8, 9, 11, 22, 23, 26, 37, 38, 39, 42, 44, 47, 48, 77, 79, back cover

U.S. Naval Historical Center, U.S. Navy: pp. 14, 16, 17, 21, 25, 29, 34, 53, 55, 56, 57, 63, 64, 65, 66, 67, 69, 72

U-boat Archiv, Cuxhaven-Altenbruch, Germany: Front cover left, 18, 21, 33

Author's collection: pp. 2, upper 6, 41

For more information on Camp Ruston, visit the Special Collections Department of the Prescott Memorial Library at Louisiana Tech University and the Louisiana Military Museum in Ruston.

The Louisiana Tech collection contains hundreds of photographs and documents, POW uniforms, furniture and crafts constructed by POWs and items from the camp hospital and archeological digs.

The collection's photographs are available via the Louisiana Digital Library at:

http://louisdl.louislibraries.org/CMPRT/Pages/home.html

Windmill constructed by Camp Ruston prisoners

THE AUTHOR

Stirred by his grandmother's stories of her family's early days in north Louisiana, **Wesley Harris** began studying local history at the age of eleven. He collected boxes of material and conducted independent study projects on local history while attending high school.

A native of Ruston, Harris earned a B.S. in Education and a Master of Arts in Human Relations and Supervision from Louisiana Tech University.

In 1977, he was hired by the City of Ruston and spent twelve years with the police department, serving as an investigator, patrol team supervisor, and finally as the agency's first training and public education director. After working for police departments in Georgia and Texas for thirteen years, Harris returned to home to Ruston in 2002 and remains in local law enforcement.

Harris is the author of several books and articles on police procedures and north Louisiana history. He can be contacted at roughedge57@yahoo.com.

Camp Ruston

**The hospital complex is to the left and prisoner compounds
to the right past the fence**

ORDER FORM

**To order additional copies of "Fish Out of Water,"
send check or money order to:**

RoughEdge Publications

P O Box 30

Ruston, LA   71273-0030

Number of copies _____ **@ $10.95 each = $**_____

Shipping & handling   **= $**_____
 (3.00 per first book, $2.00 for each
  additional book)

TOTAL   **$**_____

Please provide your mailing address:

_____

_____

_____